Ice Cream in My Refrigerator

Dr. Anita Williams Faoye

B|K
ROYSTON
Publishing

BK Royston Publishing
P. O. Box 4321
Jeffersonville, IN 47131
http://www.bkroystonpublishing.com
bkroystonpublishing@gmail.com

Cover Design: Elite Cover Designs

ISBN-13: 978-1-963136-04-3

King James Version Scriptural Text – Public Domain

Printed in the United States of America

DEDICATION

I would like to dedicate this book to my late loving grandma: Willie Ruth Hutchens Aka "Princess Little Ruth"

My Mother: Ruth Terrell Lowe. Thank you for being my mother and teaching me how to live independently in this world.

Sister: the late Ethel Elizabeth Malone Cole who was such an encourager to me down through my struggles.

My daughter: LaToya Williams Grace who has been with me through the hardships of life.

My son-in-law: LaVenice J. Grace who has stepped in as the man of our family.

My grandson: Tre'Vonte Grace who is the sunshine in my life.

My Awesome Church Family: The Church of the Kingdom of God, Hawkinsville, Georgia

My beloved assistant pastor: the late Pastor Kemuel Taylor who remained a beacon of light in dark shadow.

My angel: Richard B. Faoye who gave me the love I always wanted.

Pictorial Gallery

Mother Willie Ruth Hutchens

Ruth Terrell Lowe

Richard Faoye

LaToya Williams Grace

LaVenice J. Grace

Tre'Vonte Grace

The Late Pastor Kemuel Taylor

The Church of the
Kingdom of God

TABLE OF CONTENTS

INTRODUCTION

I want to encourage you not to focus on the struggles but focus on where you want to go and how you are going to get there. You must remember all roads have experiences, detours, some bumps, potholes, and some road closings. Sometimes you might run out of gas or have navigation trouble. You must learn to navigate through all of these tribulations.

You must learn to pull yourself out of dark places, insecurities, betrayal, heartaches. You will have to go through these struggles to get to where you want to be. Struggles are not designed for you not to get through but only to slow you up. Think positive and remind yourself that this struggle you are going through — "God is going to show you just what to do. You are not in this struggle alone. You are going to make it."

Let people misunderstand you; let them gossip about you. What they think of you is not your problem. Be proud of who you are in the midst of your struggles.

You might be faced with nightmares as dark as midnight, but if you go through it will only make you strong.

You must strive to shape yourself into a better version of who you were yesterday.

The Beginning

As a little girl, I suffered from wanting to belong, to be loved, and to have what I was taught God said I could have.

I wanted to know what I had to do to have what the word of God said I could have.

I listened thoroughly to what the preacher was ministering because I wanted so much to be successful both naturally and spiritually. I felt that the only way that would happen was to believe what the word of God said.

I remember not watching certain movies because the actors were divorced. I did not like my stepfather because of what I was being taught about having only one wife or husband. I did not have a true meaning at that time of what the word meant, all I knew was I wanted to live the life God taught in his word.

I lived in an old wood frame house with three bedrooms, a living room that served a dual role: a living room and a bedroom, a kitchen, and a back porch. The bathroom was located on the back porch with no heat in the winter. You would have to turn on the hot water to heat the bathroom so you could take a bath.

My grandmother was a sweet loving woman who dedicated her life to the church. She gave up everything just to follow the Lord.

I remember her being a very fair skinned Black woman. Of course, she could have passed for white. I was told she was of French descent. She had to get married at age 13 to take care of her husband and his small children. Their mother had died, so my grandmother was chosen to marry him to take care of them. To this union, two more children were born. After his death, she decided not to marry again.

My uncle Buddy, her son, was a black radical. They were living in Bainbridge, Georgia. Uncle Buddy would not work on a farm without being paid what he thought he should have been paid. Being the radical that he was, he threatened to kill the farmer about his pay. The farmer threatened to kill him if he asked him about any more money. He was put on the back of a horse and buggy covered with straw and dropped off in Albany, Georgia.

After living in Albany for a while, he got into trouble again and had to be shipped out of Albany hiding in a funeral home hearse.

Notes

_____

_____

_____

_____

_____

_____

_____

_____

_____

_____

_____

_____

_____

_____

_____

_____

_____

_____

Bargains

My grandmother met a divine, tongue talking, Holy Ghost filled preacher that changed her life forever.

When my grandmother moved to become the housekeeper at the church parsonage, her bedroom at our house became available. My mother moved into her room which freed up the living room.

The carpet on the floor had holes in front of each chair, the furniture had holes on all of the armrests. I do not remember how old that furniture was, but I was ashamed of it.

I was so ashamed of our house that I never invited any friends over. When they would ask if they could come over, I would always tell them that my mother did not let us receive company.

We used coal heat to warm the house. I remember my brother and I running behind the coal truck to buy coal for the heater.

I had two brothers who lived in the house with us. My older sister always stayed with her father until she got married.

Even though I had two brothers, my mother would always wake me up to make the fire. I could not understand why she made me make the fire. One day I got up enough nerve to ask her why I had to make the fire every day. She replied by saying, "you make a better fire."

Let me mention here that my mother made me carry my brother's paper route, and I had to give him half of the money. Her explanation for that was it was his paper route.

As a child, I felt mistreated and not loved. I was always blackmailed by my brothers. They knew I did not like to receive corporal punishment, so I would do their work. My mother would punish all of us if the work was not done. Even if she knew who did not do what they were supposed to do, she would whip all of us with an ironing cord and I would always be the first one. By the time she got to the youngest one, he only got a few licks because she would be tired by then. I got the most licks because I would always be first.

One day I decided that I was not going to let her spank me, so I ran away. Where did I go? To the cemetery. I roamed around the cemetery until dark. I headed back home because I had nowhere to go. It was dust dark so I peeped into the window and I saw my mother crying. She was saying she wondered where I was, and she should not have been so forceful because she knew I was a sweet daughter. When I heard her say that, I wanted her to know I was out there so I scratched on the window. My mother's boyfriend heard it. He slipped out of the room and came to the end of the house and whistled. I looked up and tried to run again, but he caught me.

He took me into the house to my mother. She sat me down and explained to me that she was hard on me because she did not want me to end up like her, depending on a man to take care of her. She said to me, "you are a strong, hard worker, and you will be successful if you continue to work hard, stay in school and get an education."

I always pretended to have more than what we had. I associated with children whose parents were teachers or their fathers worked on the railroad. They had beautiful clothes and kept money in their pockets.

To have money, I did my brother's paper route, raked yards, ran errands for neighbors, and babysat for black mothers only.

My next-door neighbor was an elementary school teacher. She would take me downtown to the clothing store and buy me five dresses for school every year. My neighbor across the street would buy me a pair of shoes.

I would hand wash my clothes to make sure they held up for a few years. That gave me the opportunity to change into something different every 14 days.

I had the nerve to enter a city-wide beauty pageant. My mother said to me, "I know you are not going up there and make a fool of yourself." So, she would not go. I did not win, but I was happy just to be in the contest.

Gaining weight was not an option for me. One, we had very little to eat and two, I had to maintain the same size so my clothes would always fit.

The husband across the street (of the neighbors that I mentioned earlier) bought the groceries for the week. On Fridays, his wife would call me over to their house to get ice cream because her husband would have purchased a new container of ice cream, and she gave the old one to us. Because we had little money for the month, we didn't buy ice cream, only the necessities for the month. Ice cream was a luxury my mother couldn't afford.

Because we had little food and it was scarce, I ate very fast because if my brother finished before I did and he wanted more, I would have to share my food with him. So, I started eating fast so I would beat him eating. I still eat fast today.

My mother would give me $5.00 to do the grocery shopping. I remember seeing one of my classmates and his mother, who was a teacher, in the grocery store. He saw the amount of food I had in the buggy and he said to me, "is that all the food you are going to buy?"

My job was to find bargains so I would roam around the store to make sure I found enough food to last for the week. My mother would say to me, "I do not know how you do it, but thanks."

After dinner on Fridays, I would sit on the porch with my ice cream from the neighbors across the street and promise myself, "one day I will be able to afford to buy all of the ice cream I want and store it in my own refrigerator."

Notes

_____

_____

_____

_____

_____

_____

_____

_____

_____

_____

_____

_____

_____

_____

_____

_____

My Grandmother,
the Church Mother

I want to talk more about members of my family.

My grandmother is the one I model my life after. She was kind, loving, caring and — most of all — a dedicated woman of God. I saved a picture of her because she wore all white, every day from her head to her toes. I asked her why one day. She replied, "this is a symbol of purity, cleanness, and righteousness." She was a dedicated woman of God who lived and personified the life of purity.

My grandmother married at age 13 to raise her husband's children. To this union she had two children of her own.

She introduced me to The Church Of The Kingdom Of God. I loved going to church with her, clapping hands, yelling praises to God, and making a joyful noise to him. We traveled with this church to conventions, fellowship services, etc. Our means of transportation was riding on the back of a big truck with a canvas over it. The church's wood benches were put on the side and front of the back of the truck. Mothers of the church would have cooked a full course meal: collard greens, potato salad, fried chicken, bean, corn bread and cake, with tea. I had the time of my life riding on the back of that truck for at least eight hours or more. We would stop on the side of the road and go into the woods to use the bathroom: men on one side of the road and women on the other side of the road. For many years, my grandmother would open the suitcase, and that was my seat. All the way from Albany, Georgia, to Eustis, Florida, and sometimes Tampa, Clearwater, Bartow, Pierce, Gainesville. I had so much fun, felt so much love, and the food was always so good.

This church at the General Assembly that was held in Douglas, Georgia, would have a banquet on that Saturday night. The food — you name it — would pass by you to make your selection. I never saw so much food at one gathering. All kinds of vegetables, mac and cheese, rice, potatoes, candied yams, string beans, steak, chicken, turkey, ham, all kind of cakes, pies, ice cream, etc. Yes, yes, yes. I never saw so much food. We could eat as much as we wanted to but could not be wasteful.

When it was time for the bishop to come to Albany for service on the fourth Sunday, I would make my way to the church parsonage because that was where my grandmother was staying. It was the only black church in Albany that had a parsonage and living quarters for saints to stay when they came to Albany. My grandmother stayed there to keep the place up. It was a large two-story building with about eight bedrooms and two bathrooms. Downstairs were the kitchen and dining room that could sit up to 75 people. Since my grandmother was the keeper of the parsonage, I would go over to help her make sure everything was ready for the bishop, his wife, and the saints that came with him.

When it was time to eat and everyone was in the dining hall, I would not sit at the dining table but would be close by. Bishop would ask me to have some dinner. I would always say, "no, thank you" because my mother taught me to say, "no, thank you" if anyone offered me any food. I would say, "no, thank you," praying they would ask me again. Of course, bishop would tell the helpers to put an extra seat at the table and fix me a plate. Oh boy! My face would light up and I would just thank God in my heart for all the blessings he was allowing me to have.

I said to myself I would never leave this church. This was heaven.

My mother's sister, my aunt left Albany (Georgia) and moved to "New York City" and passed as a white female. She called my mother and informed her that she was going to marry a white man and they could no longer have contact.

I never met my aunt, and my mother never heard from her again.

When I would spend the night with my grandmother, I could not sleep because she would moan and cry out to the Lord almost all night. She would get up and anoint my head, and prayed that the Lord would keep me from all evil. I would hear her say, "Lord bless my granddaughter. Anoint her, keep her, protect her, guide her all the days of her life."

My grandmother died my first year of college. Later in this book, I will discuss the struggle of trying to continue without her.

Mother

My mother was a beautiful light-skinned lady. She left my father in New York City when I was about five years old. She did not like my father's lifestyle, so she decided to return to Albany with two children.

Mother went to a quiet Baptist church where if you said, "amen!" or "hallelujah!" everyone would look at you to say be quiet. Grandmother, on the other hand, was at the loud holiness church. I picked up the habit of being loud in church by saying, "hallelujah!" and "amen!" from my grandmother's church, and my mother's quiet church did not allow that. So, they asked my mother not to bring me to church with her if she couldn't stop me from talking out loud. I stopped going to church with my mother. I just couldn't keep silent, and she couldn't make me stop praising my God. I was about eight or nine years old.

Every week my mother would get a money order from Western Union. My father would send her money to take care of us. My mother at that time did not have to work.

All of a sudden, the money stopped. My daddy stopped calling, and I could not figure out why. My mother was not working and that's when the hardship started. I would ask my mother why he was not sending money any more, she would say he was in the hospital. Later I found out that he was in prison. I loved my daddy and I thought my mother was being unfair to him when she started dating other men. All she would do is sit on the porch and look pretty.

One day one of the neighbors called me to come and scratch her hair. While I was scratching her, she asked me why my mother did not go anywhere. "Is it because she only has that one dress that she sits on the porch in?"

Boy, did that hurt me. I told my mother what the lady had asked me and I think that was what drove my mother to find a job.

She started working for a rich insurance agent. They did a lot for us. At Xmas time they bought gifts and gave them to my mother for us.

That lasted for a few years. My mother's employer had one child. Sometimes she would babysit at night for them. The employer wanted me to come and babysit for them after my mother got off from work. She would always say, "no," and I could not understand for the life of me why she would not let me babysit for them. She said to me, "as long as I live, I will never let you babysit for anyone." I did not understand then, but I do now. She was not going to put me in a position to be molested by a white man.

My mother was making $20 dollars a week. I thought things were going to be better, but the city was going to pave the street. Each homeowner had to pay for the driveway to be done. That really hurt our situation. She had to pay $11 a month to have that done. The money went flying out of the door.

We had four pecan trees in our yard. We made money from those pecan trees. Especially the side tree. That money was shared with us to go to the fair that came only once a year. We would walk to the fairgrounds from where I lived. It was about five miles. I do not know how we did that.

I remember when Martin Luther King, Jr., came to Albany. I was very excited about being a part of the demonstration. My mother told me and my brother not to participate because she was not coming to get us out of jail. I went any way and I was arrested by Chief Pritchett. I was so scared because I did not know how I was going to get out of jail.

All of the mattresses were taken out of the cells. We were served old rice with fatback grease and a piece of bread. I sat praying, wondering how I was going to get out. They separated me from my brother. One of the ministers whose church I played for heard that a lot of the students from Monroe High had gotten arrested. He went by my mother's house. She told him I was in that group that had gotten arrested. He came down and got me and my brother out of jail.

My neighbor that always wanted me to scratch her hair. She called me again to scratch her hair. She asked me, "Why do you always have your head in a book? Don't you know you will never be nothing? Your mother is nothing, your father is nothing. What makes you think you will be something?" At that time, something rose up in me and I said to me, I will be somebody and I will prove that to you. I am going to come back to let you know I am somebody.

I had two brothers; one was older and one younger. My older brother was the one I looked up to. When we went to games or the team center, he always kept an eye on me. I remember coming home one night from the team center. I wanted my friend to walk me home. My brother wanted to walk his girlfriend home. She lived about five miles from us. He told my friend he could walk me home, but I could not get home before he got back from walking his girlfriend home. We walked very slow home. We decided to wait on the corner until my brother got back from walking his girlfriend home. We were standing on the corner waiting my little friend decided he wanted to kiss me. After the kiss I looked up and I could see my neighbor calling my name from her front porch. Lordy, lordy what I was going to do. When my brother got back, I told him what had happen. We knew she was going to tell so we decided to pretend it did not happen.

She waited two weeks to tell my mother. The attitude my mother took was surprising. She simply told me not to do anything like that in the streets any more. Just think, I went to bed with three pairs of pants on because I thought my mother was going to spank me!

Notes

_____

_____

_____

_____

_____

_____

_____

_____

_____

_____

_____

_____

_____

_____

_____

_____

Musician for Money

To make money to help support the things I had to do, I learned to play the piano. I took music lessons from a professional music teacher. When I was in New York, I was hit by a Greyhound bus. If we were having a hardship, my father could get money from the trust that was set up for me from the accident. My mother paid for me to take lessons until the money ran out. I loved playing the piano, so I started teaching myself to play by ear rather than by note, which opened up more doors of opportunity. I got a job playing for a church in the country. The preacher would come by to get me to take me to choir rehearsal. My mother told me not to get in the front seat but sit in the back seat. My younger brother would go with us during the rehearsal nights. He would always beg me to sit in the front seat with them. He would say, "You are going freeze sitting back there. Get in the front seat with us." I never would.

My biggest problem with playing for church was the pastors who always wanted to get "fresh" with me or take advantage of me in some way. I had to take my brother with me in the car for safety because of the advances of the preachers. We didn't have a car, so I relied on them to get back and forth to rehearsals and to ultimately get paid for the work so that I could bring money into the house and may be able to buy some ice cream.

I got a better job playing for a larger church. This pastor was the same. He would always tell me how beautiful I was and if I would be his woman, he would pay me well. I told my mother so she decided to confront him about it. Of course, he denied it. My mother told him I could not play for his church unless his wife went with us to rehearsal. So, his wife accompanied us to rehearsal so that I could still play for the church. After I became a pastor, which I will talk about later, I didn't have to play anymore. God has blessed me with musicians and singers to move the music ministry forward.

Notes

_____

_____

_____

_____

_____

_____

_____

_____

_____

_____

_____

_____

_____

_____

_____

_____

_____

Tragedy Strikes

My brother and his friends, who were our neighbors, were coming home from Sylvester, Georgia. Lights on the car stopped working, and they ran into the back of a track trailer truck. One of the boys was killed. My brother and the other guy survived. All the high school students were so shocked and saddened at his death.

My brother finished school; he went into the army and fought in the Vietnam War. He fell in love with a girl from Albany who was attending Benedict College in Carolina. When he got out of the army, he went to Carolina, and next thing I knew she was in New York with him.

I must say, I am very close to my sister-in-law. My brother has passed, but she is still one of my closest friends. My brother had four girls, all who are very successful.

Before my brother passed, he came to Albany with his wife for his wife's niece's funeral. He also came to his wife's family reunion and spent two weeks with me after he had retired.

Those last visits with him were awesome. He was an alcoholic, but I was a little relaxed with my disapproval. I learned that my family had those genes, and unless God healed them of that disease it was not going to happen.

All of my family on my father's side were alcoholics: my father, brothers, uncles, aunts, and cousins. I thank God that I decided that I did not want to be one of those statistics who suffer with that illness. In my quest for success, I decided never to touch alcohol.

My young brother was a nightmare to me. He stayed in trouble and my mother catered to him. He would take our items and sell them. He was always begging for money, even if he had a hundred dollars in his pocket.

My mother wanted me to promise her that I would always see to it that he had a place to stay and food to eat. At that time, I could not buy into that because he was healthy and was one of the greatest painters in Albany. He chose not to work, and I chose not to take care of a healthy individual.

Whenever he got into trouble, he would always have the police, detective, or doctors call me. I will never forget the time he had the hospital call me to verify that he had a mental problem. He had beat up his girlfriend and when the police came, he played crazy. He had them call me so I said to the doctor, "yes, he has a mental problem." They took him to Thomasville. They put him through a series of test only to find out that he did not have a mental problem. The hospital called me to pick him up. I refused to do so. I think that was the first time I refused to let someone take advantage of me or use me.

The story goes on with my younger brother, from buying a house for him to live in, to have to plead my case with the detectives because he was stealing electricity. The house was given to him, but I took my name off the property and added his girlfriend to it.

Marry to Escape

I wanted so much to get a degree that I got married thinking things were going to get better for me. Oh, was I wrong. He was a hard worker, but he felt that one of his responsibilities was to help support his sister who was married to a man who had two families. When we got married, we moved in with his sister. It was supposed to be for six months, but it ended up being more than that. I complained so much that he bought a two-bedroom house that was a nice start-up home, but I could tell in his conversation that this was it for him.

I needed money for school, so I begged him to let me go to New York to work for the summer. I stayed with one of my friends. We went to elementary through high school together as best friends. I worked so hard going from company to company, working as a temporary operator.

I had received training working as one of the first blacks to be hired as operator at Southern Bell. I made enough money to pay for my college expenses for a year. I sent all the money to him, thinking he would save it for me. When I got home, I found out that he had spent all of the money, and I did not have any money to register for school.

I did not have a job, and I was so upset that I did not know what to do. I went to his sister to find out that they had been talking to him about my going to college. They felt like I did not need to go but should get a job.

I ran out of the house crying and ended up at a bank. I went in with no job but asking for favor. For some reason, the banker lent me the money I needed for one semester, which was $200. I would work odd jobs just to get money to pay the bank back. I got the $200 to pay it back before the next semester started and had saved enough money for the tuition for the next semester. I worked the night shift at what was then Southern Bell. Hard work, saving, and discipline helped me move toward my dream of an education.

I was able to stay working at Southern Bell for three years and was almost done with my college education but had to make choices between working, finishing school and moving forward with my life.

Notes

_____

_____

_____

_____

_____

_____

_____

_____

_____

_____

_____

_____

_____

_____

_____

_____

_____

_____

Choices

My husband was a very abusive man. He didn't start out being abusive, but six months after our marriage, it started. After I got the money from the bank, his quiet spirit turned into rage. He would be angry over the slightest thing. Sometimes I didn't really know why he was angry, but if someone, especially if it was a man, would say that he knew me, he would assume I had dated him or had had a relationship with him. He would come in and jump on me for no reason. He would check the mileage on the car every morning; if I went five miles over, he would jump on me and beat me as if I was with another man. I took that abuse for years. If we were in the car, he would drive over a hundred miles an hour just to frighten me.

I worked all night and went to school in the day. I also made sure I cooked, cleaned house, washed clothes, and did everything a housewife would do. He was always comparing me to his sister who never held a job a day in her life. I always had a drive for more and to achieve. I wanted to get it on my own and not be depending on anyone else. I thought he wanted it, too, but the abuse was too much for me. I had had enough.

At that time, I still played for churches. When it was time for me to go to choir rehearsal, he would just out of the clear blue-sky start hitting me with a belt that left welts on my skin. I had to put on a sweater in the summertime to hide the welts on my skin! I guess it was so noticeable that the choir director said to me, "If you need to talk, I am available."

By now, in my last year of college, I got a job in Midway, Alabama. Fortunately, the distance from where I lived with my husband was 150 miles. So, I got some rest from him, but I still, like a good wife, came home on weekends. The job I had in Midway, Alabama, hired me before I finished school. I took off a quarter from working to complete my hours for graduation. After graduation, thank God, I went back to the job in Midway for one year. By this time, I had a degree and a job. I was now fed up with the abuse, and I decided I was going to leave him for good.

One day when he left for work, I started packing my clothes to leave. While packing, I heard him drive in the driveway. I was so nervous that I put everything under the bed. He came and said he had forgotten something. When he left, I finished packing, called my mother, and asked her to come take me to the bus terminal. While sitting there, I looked up and I saw my husband pull up. I ran in the bathroom and was in there for about twenty minutes. When I looked out, he was gone. Forty-five minutes later the bus pulled up. I got on that bus headed for New York city. My father, brother, and two aunts lived there.

I had been to New York before, and I knew I did not want to live there. After the bus pulled away, I felt such a relief. I was headed to New York. I asked my mother not to tell him where I was going.

Washington, D.C. – New Life

When I got to Washington D.C., I knew this was where I wanted to be. I never made it to New York City. I had exactly $400. I got off the bus and sat in the bus terminal for 24 hours. I thought over and over again what I wanted to do. I called a friend who stayed with me for a few months while I was attending Albany State. I called her, and she and her husband came and picked me up.

This was when I could see the Lord working mighty in my life. Once I unpacked my clothes, I went walking looking for a church. I passed several holiness churches, and I would stand in front of the building and ask the Lord is this where you want me to be. I got no response. I kept walking until I came to this church, "Saint Paul Temple Church of God in Christ." I got such a strong feel as I stood in front of this church. I looked at the bulletin to see when the next service would be. It was the next day. I was excited about going to church the next day. When I came the next night, I was greeted with so much love from the pastor, his wife, and all the members.

I knew God was going to do something great in my life. I became very dedicated and accepted my call to the ministry. I prayed and asked God to give me some directions.

My plans were to get a teaching job at one of the high schools in D.C. I picked up the paper; the headline read 'the District of Columbia had hired 800 teachers too many, and there would be a big lay-off.' Here was a struggle again I had to encounter.

I was told by one of my friends to contact my senator and tell him I was away from home and needed a job.

I made an appointment with the senator from my district in Georgia. When I went into his office, I was very much intimidated by his looks. He asked me how he could help me. I told him I was from Albany, Georgia, and I needed a job. I explained to him that I had graduated from Albany State College with a BS in health and physical education. He asked me if Albany State was an accredited college and I told him yes, it was. He looked at me for a few minutes. "Go home, and I will call you," he said. "I cannot promise you anything, but I will try."

The struggle was real, but so was God. I had worked so hard because I wanted to be what man said I could not be.

Around four o'clock, I got a phone call from the senator. He said to me, "Go down to the Board of Education. I have secured a job for you."

Look at what God has done in spite of what the newspaper article read! I went down to the Board of Education office the next day and I was able to select from three schools. I chose Anacostia High School because it was walking distance from where I lived.

You cannot give up because you encounter struggles. Keep the dream before you at all times!

I was able to buy chocolate, vanilla, and strawberry ice cream to go in my refrigerator. I had a bathroom in my beautiful apartment. This was just the beginning of success for me.

When I signed my contract, I was told I had five years to get a master's degree in order to continue to teach high school.

Every pay period I had to send my mother $75 dollars. I did not want to do that because I felt like I needed every penny I made to survive. Of course, if I did not send it to her, she would call me, "bless me out" and hang up the phone.

After teaching for one year, I got the opportunity to register at American University. Another struggle: I needed $500 at registration. Lord where was I going to get that money from? I was casually talking to my mother about the opportunity I was offered. She said to me, "That money you sent me every month, I put it up for you. So, I will send you the $500." Look how God provided for me again!

I enrolled at American University in the field of education. Two years later, I walked away with honors and a master's degree in education with a specialty in health and physical education. My comprehensive exam was hard but easy. Does that make sense? Let me help you out. Every question, I asked the Holy Ghost to guide my mind and my fingers. I began to write about things I knew nothing about. It was unbelievable. When I would answer a question, I would say, where did this come from? I do not remember reading or studying this. God guided my thoughts and my thinking.

My advisor at that time tried very hard to get me to continue and enroll in the doctoral program.

There were people in the church whom I looked up to. They were fine dressers and looked good in their clothes. That was another goal of mine. I wanted to look sophisticated and smart. So, I worked hard in the area that I knew I was chosen for. I did not try to be like anyone; I wanted to develop my own style of dressing, preaching, and running a business. Whatever I wanted, I put it before the Lord. He made it happen.

Things were going so well with me. Then I got a call from my mother to please come home. She needed me there to help with my brother.

Notes

_____

_____

_____

_____

_____

_____

_____

_____

_____

_____

_____

_____

_____

_____

_____

_____

Back Home in Georgia

I returned to Albany. Six days after I returned, my mother passed away.

I felt lost and helpless. I felt stuck and could not get out of this quicksand. I made one big mistake and that was I went back to my husband. He was nice for a while, but after six months it started all over again.

The relationship lasted for only one year. I could not go through that abuse again. I immediately filed for a divorce and moved on.

Getting a teaching job in Albany was very difficult. Teaching was the field most black females did. If you got a job teaching, you held on to it until retirement.

I had two degrees but could not find a job in education. I finally interviewed for a teaching job working for the Department of Corrections.

Wanting very much to be an entrepreneur, I opened a gospel record company. It was doing okay, but not enough to support my lifestyle. While the record store was open, one Saturday a handsome young man came in to buy some music. It was love at first sight. We dated for a short period of time and got married.

Members of the church fell in love with him also and they felt that I was not the lady he needed.

Because of jealousy, they always kept negative conversations about me going. I was too materialistic; I had been married before so this was against our Bible teaching.

In spite of the negativity, I was still dedicated, dependable, and honest at what I did. At an early age, I was appointed District Missionary. A District Missionary was the first officer in Jurisdictional Supervisor's Cabinet and works cooperatively with the District Superintendent in various phases of the church work with the Women in the District.

It was at this time in my life that I saw corruption in the church. I was taught to raise money for state mother regardless of how small the church was. I spent so much of my own money because I refused to put pressure on those small churches that were in our district. The pressure was so great that I resigned as District Missionary and moved on.

One of my church members befriended me only to get close to my husband. Trusting and believing in people who claimed to be Christian was an encounter of disappointment. Once again, I enter another struggle. I was left to raise a daughter alone and worship with someone who betrayed my trust and married my husband.

It sounds like struggle was always at my door. If you want to be successful, you will have to get used to the struggle. Each struggle you go through just makes you better for the next round, and you find yourself going through without complaining and wanting to give up. You just continue to press toward the mark of a higher calling.

Through each struggle, I got stronger and God moved me to higher grounds each time. I got better and better. Struggles can make or break you. But if you kept God in your view, you will make it. There is a song that says, "every round goes higher and higher." You must keep praising God through all your struggles even when it hurts so bad.

After moving back to Albany, I opened a tax office. I was one of the first blacks in this area to find out about the electronic filing of tax returns that started in 1989. I went to the regional meeting, and I found out that I was the only black tax preparer there. I received the training, went to surrounding areas, and tried to locate as many black preparers to notify them of the change and what they had to do to get on board. Watch this struggle. After I did all of this work, finding everyone and training them, one of the people decided that she could do a better job and tried to pull all the people I had contact to transmit returns under her EIN. God allowed three faithful preparers to remain in my network that brought me great wealth.

Again, there was more ice cream in my refrigerator. I am now able to transfer my practice to my daughter who has tripled what I was able to with the business. Look at the ice cream keep pouring in!

Greatest Struggle – Pastoring

My greatest challenge of all was when I was sent to Hawkinsville by the General Board to pastor the church there. When I was appointed, I thought this was going to be a great opportunity for me. Little did I know that I was rejected by the members of this church, and other members of the organization fed the congregation a lot of untruths about me. I was so disappointed but I knew I could not stop. I could not quit, but I had to endure this hardship like a good warrior. I was so determined to prove to the Lord and the board that they had chosen a winner not a quitter. My favorite slogan is "winners never quit, and quitters never win."

The first struggle I had to conquer when I went to this church was the rumor that I stole money from the church. I never was a treasure or secretary or in a position I could steal money. I was a giver and always found ways to bless people in and out of the church. People I worked with and around me knew me as a giver. I gave my living room suite to someone who needed one. That left me without one. I was okay with that because I was obeying the Lord.

All of my adult life I was going without to make someone else happy. Because I did this, people thought I had a lot of money. I did not, but if God spoke to my spirit to do this, without question I did. I could never forget the times when I was young how my neighbor would help my mother feed and clothe us. It was the neighbor who always had ice cream to give me because my mother could never buy that for us.

I wanted so much for this church to be a model church. I would solicit funds from my co-workers and friends to help me do the things I had put in my spirit to do.

The church was sitting on block and looked terrible on the outside. But once you went inside, it looked totally different.

We were in service one Sunday and the Lord showed me a vision of a new church. I got up with a testimony of what God had shown me. When I sat down, one of the deacons got up and said, "Pastor, I have the property for this new church. I will give you the land." I was not ready for that but I knew God was working.

We only had six thousand dollars, and 45 percent of the members did not want a new church. I endured trials and tribulations to get this project done.

The General Board came down to discuss with the congregation if this was feasible at this time. The majority of the General Board felt that this project was not needed at this time. I began to pray. The bishop got up to express his desire for this new building. He made one statement that changed the hearts of the people and got a majority vote from the board. The statement was, "we preach that we are the head and not the tail," he said, "but I cannot see that when I drive up to our churches. Why not trust God and make this happen?"

The state-of-the-art church was built and 16 years later paid off.

Ice cream was once again put in my refrigerator. God also allowed me to become a member of the Church of the Kingdom General Board. And to top that I became the CEO of the Church of the Kingdom of God.

Ice cream — scoops of ice cream in my refrigerator.

Notes

_____

_____

_____

_____

_____

_____

_____

_____

_____

_____

_____

_____

_____

_____

_____

_____

_____

_____

My Guardian Angels

I met an awesome man of God who blessed me in so many different ways. He was caring, devoted, and understanding and supported the ministry in every area that he could. He always wanted to know what he could do to help. He was planning to get a group of Nigerians to start attending church with him. He was a Nigerian who came to America to get an education. He had three children: two live here in the states. He was very interested in developing a stronger relationship with his children. We had big plans for us. We were married for ten months. During that time, we traveled at least three times a month to places that we always wanted to go to. It was January when COVID hit

Albany, Georgia. We had no idea that we would be victims of that disease.

All of us worked in the tax office. My husband was the mail carrier. He delivered files to our location in Sylvester, Georgia. Everyone in the office came back expressing that they did not feel well. Since everyone in the office did not want to wear a mask, my daughter closed the office.

My husband started coughing, I took him to the doctor and he was told he had congestive heart failure. A few weeks later, he went to the hospital, and I never saw him again.

Lord, this struggle was a bit much. I lost him, my office manager, his wife, few clients, and close friends. The Lord said to me, "You've got to give me thanks." That's all I could hear him say.

The struggles are so real, but so is God. Two years later, I lost my tax partner whom I spoke to every day since 1989. We did big tax business together. He was loyal and dedicated to the practice and my church. He was like my big brother. Guess what, he got sick in the middle of the tax season and died. Lord, another big struggle but I managed to get through that.

A couple years later, my loving, dedicated, loyal, assistant pastor died at a very young age. He had been appointed to take over as Pastor the latter part of the year. This was another big disappointment, but God strengthened me through this struggle.

In the midst of that struggle, God showed me in spite of what I was going through and because I held on, he would shower me with many blessings.

Struggles are created to push you to your destiny. We want to shun struggles, but struggles only make you strong.

You have to live the shame, disappointment, agony, and heartbreaks of failure. Keep in mind that God is with you and is preparing you for the goals and dreams that were made known to you.

You must never doubt your worth or the beauty of your worth. Keep striving, keep dreaming and working day and night for the things you want. I went from the front porch of my wood frame house with a bathroom with no heat on the back porch of the house to a four-bedroom house with four bathrooms and a refrigerator with all the ice cream I want. I have money in the bank, a successful tax practice, a beautiful church family and building. The church is debt free. My daughter, son-in-law and grandson are all working through their struggles but encouraged to keep working for the goals they have and desire.

I have been taught some tough times and have fought my battles like a warrior. I was not fighting battles for myself, but making sure I was a perfect example of encouragement on how to endure hardness as a good solider. If you go through your struggles you will win. If you quit, you lose.

Notes

_____

_____

_____

_____

_____

_____

_____

_____

_____

_____

_____

_____

_____

_____

_____

_____

_____

About the Author
Pastor, Dr. Anita Williams Faoye

Pastor Faoye was born in New York City and reared in Albany, Ga. She received a B.S. degree (Albany State), a M.Ed. (The American University), and a Doctorate degree in curriculum and instruction (University of Sarasota). She retired as assistant principal of Dougherty Middle School. She served as School Board At-Large for Four years for Dougherty County School System. She runs a successful tax and book-keeping business. She has one daughter, LaToya Williams Grace, a son-in-law, LaVenice J. Grace, and a grandson, Tre'Vonte Grace.

Pastor Faoye knew that God had a special call on her life at an early age. She spent time serving in the Church of God in Christ, as a Minister of Music and on the Missionary Board, under the leadership of Bishop J.H. Dell. Pastor Faoye felt the desire to work in the church where she was reared, so she made the decision to return to The Church of the Kingdom of God. She received her first pastoral appointment under the leadership of Bishop William H. Bryant, Jr. as Co–Pastor in Dawson, GA.

Dr. Anita Williams-Faoye has served tirelessly and faithfully as Pastor in Hawkinsville, Georgia, since 1997. Under her visionary leadership, the church has grown both spiritually and naturally. Pastor Faoye directed the addition of a Social Hall to the old Worship Facility and in 2007, the construction of a beautiful new Multi-Purpose Worship Facility and Social Hall. Along with her Pastoral role in Hawkinsville, Pastor Faoye also served as General Women's President under the leadership of Bishop Willie J. Toomer.

Pastor Faoye's recent work in foreign missions has resulted in the construction of the first Church of the Kingdom of God in Ghana, West Africa. Her role as a leader and visionary have also led to the purchase of new church bus and community give aways in partnership with The Middle Georgia Food Bank and World Vision. Pastor Faoye has served faithfully on the General Board of Elders and is currently the CEO of The Church of the Kingdom of God, Inc.

Notes

_____

_____

_____

_____

_____

_____

_____

_____

_____

_____

_____

_____

_____

_____

_____

_____

_____

_____